A
VIRGINIAN
INDIAN

Contents

Introduction

This book tells the story of Matoax, an American Indian princess, who lived from about 1595 until 1617. Matoax means 'little snow feather'. She also had another name, Pocahontas, and it is by this name that she is usually remembered. She was the daughter of the great Chief Powhatan, who ruled over a large number of tribes and villages in south-eastern America, in the state now called Virginia. He was a wise ruler and a brave warrior, who governed his people with the help of local chiefs and shamans, or priests.

In 1607, three ships appeared on the great river which ran through Powhatan's territory. They brought men who seemed very strange and threatening to the Indians. These 'strangers' had pale skins, wore peculiar clothes, carried dangerous 'thundersticks', or guns, and spoke an incomprehensible language. It also seemed, to the Indians, that they were trying to take over their land.

The strangers were not very skilled at farming or hunting, and chose an unhealthy site on which to build their settlement. Soon they fell ill, and were in danger of starving to death. But Matoax was very curious about them, and wanted to learn all she could about their way of life. She also felt very sorry for them, and wanted to help them. What happened next is told in this book.

This book is based on a true story, and you can find out what happened to Matoax when she grew up by turning to page 30. At the end of the book, you will also find more pictures of Virginian Indians and their way of life. There are also some ideas for places to visit and books to read.

The Looking Hill

'Come with me!' said Matoax. 'I'm going to find out what's going on down by the river!'

Her cousin, Namontack, looked doubtful.

'If I come with you I'll miss the hunt,' he said.

'You can go hunting any day,' replied Matoax, rather scornfully. 'This will be much more interesting, I promise you! You'll see!'

Namontack couldn't make up his mind. He had been looking forward for a long time to going hunting with the great Chief Powhatan, who was visiting Namontack's village. He had arrived a few days ago, bringing a bodyguard with him, and many of his wives and children too, and lots of servants to look after them. There had been feasting and dancing, and today they were planning a hunt.

'Hurry up!' Matoax called impatiently. She was Powhatan's favourite daughter so she was used to getting her own way. With a sigh, Namontack got up and followed her.

6

They set off up the narrow forest track which led to the top of the Looking Hill. From there, they could look down into the next valley. In the distance, sunlight glittered on the river as it flowed away towards the sea.

'Look!' cried Matoax. 'There they are!'

Namontack shaded his eyes against the sun. He could just make out a little cluster of buildings – not proper wigwams, for they were oddly-shaped and made of logs and turf. Strange-shaped boats floated near the river bank, and woodsmoke curled upwards from an untidy bonfire. Then he saw them.

'I can see creatures moving about!' he said. 'Their faces are white, like the moon! Look, that one has a metal shell around his body! And that one has yellow hair, like cornmeal.' He shivered. 'Matoax, I'm scared! Who are they? Are they evil spirits?'

'I'm not sure,' said Matoax. 'I think they may be people. But the spirits have sent them here. They're not like us!'

7

Children of the Great White Hare

The children arrived back at the village late in the afternoon. Namontack ran off to find the hunters; Matoax joined some women who were weaving mats and baskets out of reeds. She sat down next to her aunt, Chief Winganucki, and began idly sorting turkey feathers into sizes, for making a feather cape. Winganucki was a famous storyteller. She knew all the secret stories belonging to their tribe.

'I'll tell you the story of Manitou's daughter,' she said to the women.

'Manitou, the Great Spirit, made all things. First he made a woman, and then he made a man. Their children became hunters in the forest. One day in winter, some hunters came across Manitou's daughter, fast asleep in a hidden valley. She told them to return to the valley in summertime. When they came back, to their amazement they found the whole valley transformed. Corn was growing where her right hand had touched the earth, beans sprouted where her left hand had lain, and tobacco where her

feet had rested. And now those plants are Manitou's greatest gifts to our people.'

'Aunt, did the Great Spirit make all tribes the same?' asked Matoax. She was thinking of the strange people she had seen down by the river.

'We are all the children of the Great White Hare, and our ancestors lived in the sky world with him before they came down to Earth,' replied Winganucki. 'In those days, the Earth was cold and unfriendly, so the Great White Hare brought fire down from the sky to keep us warm.'

'Could new people come down from the sky now, as our tribe did?' asked Matoax. Perhaps that was where the strangers came from!

Her aunt laughed. 'Child, you are like the frog who wanted to know about everything. It went exploring and jumped down a duck's throat. It got eaten alive, and too much curiosity will get you into trouble too!'

Matoax asked no more questions, but she couldn't stop thinking about the strangers.

'Even if nobody here will tell me about them,' she said to herself, 'Sooner or later, I'm going to find out! Just wait and see!'

9

The Pow-wow

The next day, chieftains from all the tribes which lived near by arrived in the village.

'Father has summoned them to a pow-wow,' Matoax told Namontack. 'That means they have something important to discuss. Perhaps it's the strangers down by the river! Let's listen and find out!'

They crept round to the back of the great wigwam. Through a little gap in the wall of reed matting they could see the chieftains seated on benches. A shaman sprinkled a circle of tobacco round the fire.

'He's doing that to make the spirits listen,' whispered Matoax. 'He's a very wise man who knows all about medicine and magic.'

The shaman danced round the fire, calling to the spirits in a strange, high-pitched voice.

'The spirits have spoken! Remember!' he cried. 'Remember, Great Powhatan, the prophecy that foretold the coming of the white strangers! Twice they will be driven away, but the third time they will defeat you. Now is their third visit, Great Powhatan! Beware!'

'I am not frightened by this prophecy,' replied Powhatan proudly. 'My warriors could kill all these men, if I commanded it!'

Chief Winganucki spoke next. 'I think these strangers have come to trade, not to fight,' she said.

Then Powhatan's brother, Opachank, leapt up. He was a very fierce and warlike chief. 'They are not traders,' he shouted. 'They have weapons that shoot deadly thunderbolts. They have come to steal our land. We must destroy them now!'

'I have a better plan,' said Powhatan. 'These people will need food, and we have seen what bad hunters they are. They will starve unless we let them share our crops. In return for food, we will make them do exactly what we want. If they are good men they could be useful to us. They could help us fight our enemies with their thundersticks. But we will watch them, and if they take our land we will destroy them!'

Opachank scowled, but all the other chiefs agreed with Powhatan.

At Werowocomoco

Matoax had hoped that her father would take her to meet the strangers. She was very disappointed when she realised that he did not mean to visit them.

'Great Chief Powhatan does not visit mere traders,' he announced. 'I shall wait for them to come to me!'

'But I want to find out more about them,' Matoax said to herself. 'And some day I will!'

For the moment, however, she was bored. After visiting all his chiefs in their villages, Powhatan returned to his own village of Werowocomoco. He had left instructions that all the chiefs were to keep a close watch on the strangers, and to send him reports on all they did. Matoax often went down to the river, hoping to meet a messenger bringing news of the strange people.

On other days, she would walk through the fields where the women were weeding the young corn. Because she was a princess, she did not work in the fields. She often went to talk to the scarecrow boy, who sat on a platform in the middle of the growing corn and clapped his hands to drive away the birds. He was always glad of someone to talk to. His was a lonely and boring job, but he knew how important it was. 'If the birds eat the corn, then we'll all go hungry next winter!' he would say.

One morning, Matoax heard the villagers chanting to the corn spirits as the women began the second sowing of corn. It was sown twice a year, in spring and in early summer. Last year, the men had started to clear a new field from the forest. They had cut a ring of bark around each tree trunk, and lit fires at the base so that the roots died. The trees had fallen over by now but it would be many years before the roots deep underground would rot away. The villagers had no tools strong enough to dig them up, so the women had scraped up little mounds of good soil in between the roots. In each mound, they planted four seeds of corn and two beans. As the corn grew, it would provide a support for the beans to climb up.

'What hard work it is,' thought Matoax. 'Perhaps I shouldn't complain about having nothing to do!'

14

The River

In the evenings, when work was over, the villagers liked to go down to the river bank. There was always something to see. The river was full of good things to eat – turtles, waterbirds and all kinds of fish – and the women often barbecued freshly-caught salmon, or roasted crabs. They were delicious!

The men had made a weir out of wooden stakes and plaited reeds, to trap the fish as they swam up the river from the sea. Once inside the weir, the fish could not escape. At low tide, when the river was shallow, it was easy to wade out and scoop them up in nets made of silk-grass.

Matoax spent whole days by the river. Sometimes she played with the village children, but more often she wandered by herself, diving from overhanging branches, swimming underwater to find mussels, or standing quietly in the shallows trying to spear fish with a pointed stick. She sometimes liked to watch the men making canoes. They hollowed out a log by setting fire to the wood along its upper length, then scraping away the scorched part with shells. Matoax knew how to paddle a canoe by herself, and how to punt it along using a long pole. She loved to follow the men when they went fishing at night. They lit fires in their canoes, and the light attracted shoals of fish towards their nets.

The river also served as a highway, linking all the villages along its banks with each other and with the sea. One day, Matoax met some traders who were travelling inland from the coast. They brought more news about the strangers. They had been cutting down trees and trying to grow crops. Instead of planting two or three seeds at a time in the good soil between the tree roots, they had thrown seed all over the ground and let it lie where it fell.

'Like that, it will never grow,' the traders said.

Matoax remembered what Powhatan had said at the pow-wow: 'They will starve unless we let them share our crops.' She felt very sorry for the strangers.

15

The Feast of the Green Corn

It was midsummer. The first crop of corn was ready for harvesting. The villagers were planning a special feast to celebrate the Festival of the Green Corn. The women were busy cooking – some were grinding corn, others were mixing the ingredients for a spicy bean stew. The men had done their share of work towards the feast two days ago, by hunting deer and catching turkeys. Soon, the women would roast these over a huge fire. There would be cornmeal cakes and juicy melons, too.

Suddenly, one of the village boys came rushing up from the river bank.

'The strange men are coming!' he gasped. 'I've seen their boats! They're getting ready to land on the river bank – it won't be long before they get up here!'

When Powhatan heard this news he came out of his royal wigwam and spoke to the excited villagers. 'We will receive these strangers as honoured guests,' he commanded. 'But no one is to sell them any corn, no

matter what they offer. Not even for their sharpest
knives, or cooking pots of copper. We must wait for
the second harvest before we can be sure that we will
have enough to feed ourselves during the winter. By
then the strangers will be so hungry that they will give
their magic weapons in exchange for food. They may
even help us fight our enemies! Now, go down to the
river and welcome them to the feast!'

Matoax rushed off with the others, and led the
strangers to the feasting place. The villagers squatted
on rows of mats, the men facing the women. When all
was ready, Powhatan and his wives joined the
gathering. Matoax was made to go and sit with the
other royal women. The feasting and dancing began.
The villagers leapt around the sacred fire, waving
corn stalks and chanting thanks to the spirits for the
new crop.

Matoax watched the strangers eagerly, but she
could not leave her place near her father. Their leader
smiled across at her. He had a golden beard and
bright blue eyes. 'He looks friendly,' she thought.
'I would like to help him.'

17

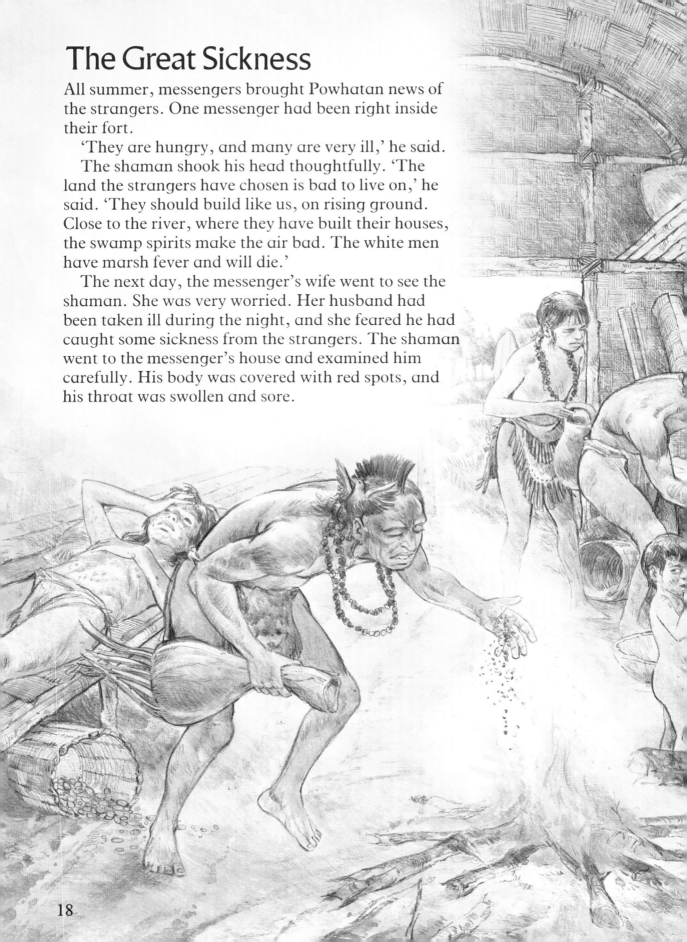

The Great Sickness

All summer, messengers brought Powhatan news of the strangers. One messenger had been right inside their fort.

'They are hungry, and many are very ill,' he said.

The shaman shook his head thoughtfully. 'The land the strangers have chosen is bad to live on,' he said. 'They should build like us, on rising ground. Close to the river, where they have built their houses, the swamp spirits make the air bad. The white men have marsh fever and will die.'

The next day, the messenger's wife went to see the shaman. She was very worried. Her husband had been taken ill during the night, and she feared he had caught some sickness from the strangers. The shaman went to the messenger's house and examined him carefully. His body was covered with red spots, and his throat was swollen and sore.

'I have never seen this sickness before,' said the shaman. 'It must be a curse brought on us by the strange men.'

There followed a terrible time for the whole village. One person after another caught the mysterious sickness and many died. Every family had someone who was ill, and often there was no one well enough to cook or to carry water. The shamans did all they could to drive the sickness away. They lit fires and burned tobacco to fill the rooms with healing scents. They made herb ointments to keep away the spirits that brought the disease. But even their skills could not prevent Matoax catching the sickness. She was very ill for several days. She lay in bed, hardly knowing or caring where she was. Her aunts nursed her back to health and, little by little, she regained her strength. Once she was better she often thought of the sick and hungry strangers. They had nobody to care for them.

At last the sickness left the village. The shamans led a procession down to the riverside and thanked the spirits for making them well again. Matoax silently prayed that the spirits would save the strangers, too.

The Deer Dance

It was the season of falling leaves, when the second corn crop was harvested. The women and the older children were busy all day, husking, shelling and drying corn so that it would keep through the winter.

At this season, the women performed the sacred Deer Dance. This year, as usual, all the villagers, except for the young women chosen as dancers, gathered on the edge of the village, close to the forest. They lit a great fire, and the musicians made a loud noise with drums and rattles. Suddenly there was the sound of wild singing in the forest. The deer dancers were coming! They rushed out of the trees into the firelight, and began the sacred dance. Their faces and movements showed that the forest spirits had entered their bodies. They sang for joy and stamped in time to the music.

As Matoax stood watching the dance, she looked across the ring of firelight and saw some pale faces in the crowd. The strangers had returned! They must have come to ask for corn once more. She was glad to see that the blue-eyed man with the yellow beard was still with them. So he had survived the mysterious sickness! She turned to watch the dance again. After a while, she realised that the strangers had disappeared. Then a voice beside her made her jump. It was Yellow Beard, and he was speaking, rather slowly and awkwardly, in her own language!

'Princess, tell me what this dancing means.'

Matoax was very pleased that he had chosen to come and talk to her.

'We are praising the spirits of the hunt,' she said. 'The women wear leaves and deer horns to call the forest spirits to come to us and bring good hunting.'

After the dance, there was feasting until late into the night. All evening, Matoax stayed beside her new friend and answered his questions.

'Tomorrow, will you come and tell me all about your country?' she asked.

'Yes, princess, I will,' he promised. Then he and the other strangers rose and made their way down to the fort by the river.

The Prisoner

At midwinter, the chieftains of many of the tribes came to Werowocomoco for the winter festival. Matoax waited impatiently for Namontack to arrive. She rushed to tell him about her new friend.

'I call him Yellow Beard,' she said. 'He comes here often and speaks our language quite well now. He has given me wonderful presents – blue beads like the sky and a shining plate which shows you your face.'

'You are wrong to like the strangers,' replied Namontack. 'Chief Opachank is sure they mean to drive us from our land. He captured some who were exploring the river and setting up crosses to mark the ground as theirs. He is bringing their leader here to be executed. Perhaps it is your Yellow Beard.'

'It can't be Yellow Beard! He is my friend and I will never let him die!' cried Matoax.

The sun was almost setting as the chieftains assembled inside the long wigwam. It was dark inside, apart from the firelight. Matoax peered anxiously in from the doorway. Her father sat, stern and grave, with his wives and the other chieftains. The shaman called on the spirits to help them make a wise decision. Then the discussion began. Many chiefs reported that the strangers had used their thundersticks to kill innocent people, and that they had tried to take over the land.

'I demand war against the strangers and death for their leader!' shouted Opachank.

All the chiefs shouted in agreement.

'Bring the prisoner in,' commanded Powhatan.

Matoax trembled as four guards led the prisoner in. With horror, she recognised Yellow Beard! The guards carried in a big stone, and put it down in front of Powhatan. Roughly, they forced the prisoner's head down on to it. The executioner raised his club.

'Stop! He is mine! He is mine!' screamed Matoax. She rushed forward and flung herself between Yellow Beard and his guards.

There was silence. Then Powhatan spoke.

'The spirits have sent this as a sign,' he said. 'My daughter claims this man as a brother. He shall be spared.'

In the Fort

Matoax was very happy. Powhatan had accepted Yellow Beard as a member of their tribe. Now he was Matoax's adopted brother, and Powhatan's adopted son. This meant that Powhatan would treat the strangers exactly like members of his own tribe.

'They need our help and we shall do all we can for them,' he said.

Yellow Beard told Powhatan and the shamans that his companions were sick and starving. Many of them were homeless too, after a fire had burnt down some of the houses.

'I must return to the fort,' said Yellow Beard, 'and tell them that help will soon reach them.'

'We shall send food,' Powhatan promised, 'and Matoax shall bring it to you.'

The next day, feeling proud and excited, Matoax set off for the fort, leading a procession of warriors and servants carrying food and medicines. Yellow Beard met them at the gate. The strangers crowded round eagerly, gazing at the food with hungry eyes. In return, one of them gave Matoax a doll, dressed in stiff, bulky clothes. Matoax was fascinated. Yellow Beard saw how she was looking at the doll's clothes, and smiled.

'All women in my country, even girls like you, wear long skirts and bodices and hats like that,' he said. 'And princesses wear especially beautiful clothes.'

'But how can they run, or dance, or play?' exclaimed Matoax. 'Look, can they do this?' She threw off her cloak and turned several cartwheels round the open square in the middle of the fort.

Suddenly, she realised that some of the men were laughing at her. She was offended, and picked up her cloak and stood very still.

'Why are they making fun of me?' she demanded.

'They don't mean to be rude,' said Yellow Beard, 'but in our country, princesses don't behave like that. Please forgive them.'

Matoax was silent. She was still angry and upset.

'Well, then,' said Yellow Beard, laughing, 'if you don't believe me, you'll just have to come to our country to see for yourself!'

Matoax Makes a Choice

As she returned home through the forest, Matoax suddenly felt doubtful. Perhaps the strangers had been laughing at her rudely and unkindly after all? Perhaps their country was not as beautiful as Yellow Beard said? Perhaps she would be too scared to travel with them across the sea? She didn't know what to think. Then she remembered something a wise shaman had said to her:

'When you need to find wisdom, listen to the voice of the Great Spirit. You can hear his voice in the silence of the forest.'

She sat down under a tall pine tree and listened to the wind in its branches. It seemed to say that no land could be richer, safer or more friendly than her own. Here, she was a royal princess, the daughter of a famous chieftain. She would soon be old enough to lead the Deer Dance and to wear a royal cloak of shining white feathers. If she went away with the strangers she might never be able to return to her family and her friends.

26

Matoax was undecided. She would certainly miss her father, Namontack and her village. Then she looked down at the strange doll in her lap. Its dress was a deep glowing colour, which she had never seen before. It was neither red nor blue, but more beautiful than either. The doll wore a frilled collar around its neck, made of something that looked like snowflakes or ferns, but finer and more delicate than any ferns she knew. What a wonderful land it must be where they could make such lovely things!

She thought, too, about Yellow Beard. He was her friend and her adopted brother. He had been kind to her. He would look after her in the strange land, and she would soon make many new friends there. She might even meet their royal princesses!

Matoax made up her mind. She would be brave. She would go with the strangers to visit their country across the sea. A new and fascinating world was waiting for her, and who could tell what wonders – or dangers – it had in store?

Picture Glossary

Captain John Smith, or 'Yellow Beard', set off from England in 1607. He hoped to find gold and silver in Virginia. Earlier Spanish explorers had found precious metals and gemstones on their journeys to countries in South America. The settlers never found gold in Virginia, but, with the help of the Indian people, they eventually learned how to grow food and trap animals, and how to survive the cold winters. The Indians also showed them how to grow tobacco, which they sent back to Europe where it became very popular. Some of them became very rich through this trade. They built a new town in Virginia, which they called Jamestown, after the king of England.

We know so much about these Indian tribes because an artist called John White travelled with an expedition in 1587. He drew many pictures of the Indians, and of their houses, clothes, boats and weapons, and also of the animals and plants that he saw. These pictures have survived until today and are the basis for some of the drawings in this book.

Above: Fortified village
The houses are made with bent saplings and are covered with bark or matting. This could be rolled up in summer to let in light and air.

Below: This map of North America shows the location of the Virginian Indians. The enlarged section shows the Indians' country in detail.

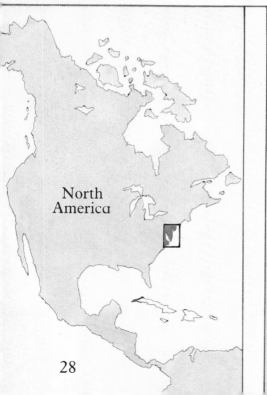

North America

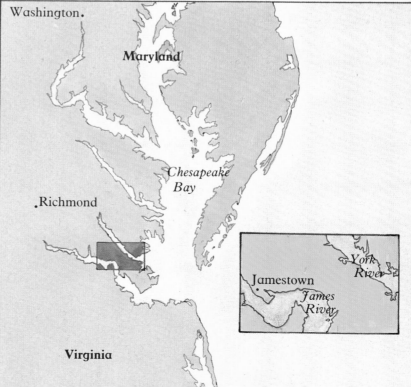

Washington

Maryland

Chesapeake Bay

Richmond

Jamestown

York River

James River

Virginia

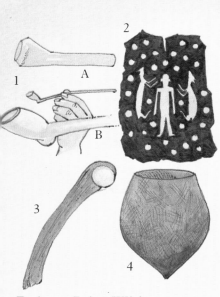

Left: Indian objects

1. Tobacco pipes
   - A Indian, usually clay. A wood or cane stem might be attached.
   - B English clay pipe, made in imitation.
2. Chieftain's deerskin cloak, decorated with shells.
3. A club was a stone wedged in the top of a piece of wood.
4. Clay cooking pot.

Below: John White produced drawings of the Indians and of the wildlife. This vivid record of the 'new' land was vital to later expeditions.

- A Indian in war paint for hunting.
- B Indian medicine man (shaman).
- C Indian woman carrying her child.

Above: Produce from America

5. Tobacco
6. Maize
7. Kidney beans
8. Pineapple
9. Sunflower
10. Cocoa
11. Capsicums
12. Squash and marrow
13. Tomato
14. Turkey

Finding Out More

Matoax, or Pocahontas, is remembered today for her kindness to the settlers, and for her bravery in defying her father when he wanted to execute her friend, Captain John Smith. The Indian people's generosity saved the settlers from starving to death when their own attempts at farming had failed. Unfortunately, this generosity meant that the strangers survived only to push the Indians off their lands, as Chief Opachank had feared.

Several years after this story ends, Matoax fell in love with one of the settlers, John Rolfe, and married him. She decided to go back to England with him, to see the strange country she had heard so much about from Captain John Smith and his companions. This was a very brave decision, since she had to face a long, dangerous and stormy voyage across the Atlantic Ocean in a cramped sailing ship. People in England were very interested to meet her, and to learn about her homeland. Sadly, while she was staying in the port of Gravesend, waiting for a ship to take her back to Virginia, she caught pneumonia and died. She was just 22 years old.

Books to Read

The following books contain information about Matoax (also called Pocahontas) and the Virginian Indians:

C. Sauer **Man in Nature** (Turtle Island Foundation 1980)

G. Woodward **Pocahontas** (University of Oklahoma Press 1969)

You may need an adult to help you read the books below and on the opposite page, but they can tell you a lot more about the life of the Virginian Indians. They also contain many pictures.

P. L. Barbour **Pocahontas and her World** (Houghton Mifflin 1969)

G. Caselli **The Renaissance and New World** (Macdonald 1985)